A MOTHER'S YEAR

HarperCollins*Publishers*
1 London Bridge Street
London SE1 9GF

www.harpercollins.co.uk

HarperCollins*Publishers*
1st Floor, Watermarque Building, Ringsend Road
Dublin 4, Ireland

First published by HarperCollins*Publishers* in 2021

1 3 5 7 9 10 8 6 4 2

Text by Emma Bastow
Design by e-Digital Design

A catalogue record for this book is available from the British Library

ISBN 978-0-00-846375-5

Printed and bound in Bosnia and Herzegovina

MIX
Paper from responsible sources
FSC™ C007454

FSC™ is a non-profit international organisation established to promote the responsible
management of the world's forests. Products carrying the FSC label are independently certified
to assure consumers that they come from forests that are managed to meet the social, economic
and ecological needs of present and future generations, and other controlled sources.

This book is produced from independently certified FSC paper
to ensure responsible forest management.
For more information visit: www.harpercollins.co.uk/green

A
MOTHER'S
YEAR

365 WRITING
PROMPTS FOR MOTHERS

About the Author

Emma Bastow has over 20 years' experience in book publishing, and is also the author of *A Writer's Year*, *A Mindful Year*, and *I Love Leopard* for HarperCollins*Publishers*. Emma lives in Brighton, East Sussex, where she can often be found lost in the pages of a book, wandering the Lanes, or skimming stones at the beach with her young son.

To my family, with thanks.

Introduction

"Congratulations, you're a mom!" These are the words you'll typically hear when first handed your precious bundle of joy. No amount of preparation or research can prepare you for the journey ahead and for the mixture of emotions you'll experience in the coming days, months, and years—anticipation, joy, trepidation, and all-consuming, heart-bursting, pure unadulterated love. At times you'll wish time could stand still so you can stay in a moment and enjoy your children exactly as they are forever. While that isn't possible, journaling can be a great tool for staying grounded, documenting the good times, and working through coping mechanisms for any challenges you may face. Here you'll explore what has surprised you about motherhood, take yourself back to that moment when you first laid eyes on your child, and have lots of fun remembering the amusing and heart-warming things your children have said and done over the years.

How to use this book

In the following pages you will find 365 prompts for every mood, with space below to note down your thoughts and feelings. You may like to work through the book methodically, allocating a little time each day to journaling. Or you might prefer to flick through the pages at random, selecting the exercises that take your fancy. Throughout the journal, we refer to your "child." However, if you have more than one child, feel free to write the prompts about all or one of your children. However you choose to use this book, be kind to yourself and move on to another prompt if an exercise doesn't feel quite right—with 365 prompts to choose from, there's bound to be an idea a few pages away that will better suit you in the moment.

Getting started

Whether you are used to journaling and are looking for further inspiration, or are just beginning to dabble, make the prompts in this book work for you. If you're feeling creative, select a story-writing prompt and let your imagination run wild. If you're in need of a calming moment, turn the pages to a mindful exercise and enjoy the relaxing sensation. And if you're in a playful mood, a fun family activity could be the order of the day. Most importantly, enjoy your year of journaling and memory-making.

Why document your year?

Do you ever find yourself thinking, "Where has the time gone?" Motherhood can be hectic. All too often we find ourselves caught up in the day to day routines of family life, and before we know it twelve months have flown by—our children are a whole year older, we're a whole year older, and many precious memories have been made. The prompts here are designed to help you to slow down and commit these moments to paper.

Some prompts are reflective, looking back at your own childhood and past experiences; others are designed to help you plan for the future; and many are just for fun, to maximize family time and really make the most of the day. So read on to begin your journaling journey and create a record of the year ahead—who knows, your own grandchildren may even read this journal one day and be inspired to create parenting journals of their own.

What made you laugh today?

Describe your parenting style in no more than ten words.

Stop what you are doing right now and look around you. Perhaps your environment is one of calm and serenity, or it may be chaos and mayhem. Take a breath and just be in this moment for a few seconds before getting on with your day. How do you feel?

Spend today taking mental photographs of family life, capturing the marvelous and the mundane, and committing these precious moments to memory. Use the space below to document your day.

Today is a Yes Day! Within reason, say "yes" to everything your child requests, then note how this made you feel. Was it liberating? Did you have fun? Could you make Yes Days part of your regular routine?

Write a love letter to yourself. Include your most attractive attributes, your greatest achievements, and your qualities as a mother.

Write a letter to your child-free self. Having experienced motherhood, would you have the same cares and worries if you could go back in time?

Look out of a window with your child. On separate pieces of paper, both draw what you can see, but don't show each other your sketches until they are finished. Are your drawings similar? Have you picked out the same objects?

Which is more desirable: intelligence or confidence?

What is your time of year and why?

Being a mom is hugely rewarding but can also be overwhelming at times. Note down five coping strategies you can employ when things start getting out of hand.

Ask your own mother or a close family member to share a recipe with you and prepare this recipe with your own child. Did you enjoy the experience?

_____

_____

_____

_____

_____

_____

_____

_____

_____

_____

_____

_____

_____

_____

_____

_____

_____

What three things would make your life easier? Are there any steps you could take to make them a reality?

How are you like your own mother or other close female family members? Do you share interests and passions?

Stand in front of a mirror with your child and study your reflections. Do your faces have any similarities? How are they different?

Sit down with your child and both write a Haiku poem about a pet or family member. Read them to each other. Whose was the funniest?

Set aside time today to really listen to your partner or a close friend without interruption or judgment, then ask them to do the same for you. How easy did you find this?

What parental responsibilities would you outsource if you could?

What is the combined age of your immediate family?

How old was your own mother when you were born? Were you older or younger when your first child came along? Note how this may have affected your experiences of motherhood.

To what extent do you feel privileged? Take a moment to talk to your child about privilege and what this means to you. Did you find this easy?

Write down your child's name vertically, with each letter on a separate line. Think of a word beginning with each letter to describe your child.

Once a week, write about a good experience in the space below. After one month, read back over your notes, reflecting on the positives of the previous weeks.

How cautious are you and how does this impact your parenting?

Who is in charge in your family?

Take a moment to note your blessings.

What scares you the most?

Do you share chores equally with the other adults in your home?

Write down ten major differences between your own childhood and that of your child. Are the differences positive?

Before bed, ask your child to tell you three good things that happened during their day and jot these down, and in return share your own three good things. Try to make this a daily ritual and note whether it alters your attitude towards "bad" days.

Write a short children's story where your child's favorite toy comes to life and goes on an adventure. Share it with your child.

Hold hands with your child. If they are older you may not have done this for a while. How does their hand feel in yours? Whose skin is smoother? Describe each other's hands in no more than three words.

Are you a naturally positive person?

Define your own childhood in one sentence.

List your top ten learning experiences since becoming a mom. What have you discovered about yourself?

On separate pieces of paper, ask your child to draw a caricature of you, really exaggerating your features. Do the same for your child. Have fun, laugh, and admire your masterpieces. Write about the experience below.

The kids are in charge! Give the decision-making over to your child for the day—let them decide what to eat, where to go, and set them a few challenges along the way. How did it go?

Take a look at a piece of art with your child (this can be in reality or a picture on your cell phone or computer). What do you see? Describe it to each other. How does it make you feel?

What was the best thing about your day?

What do you wish you had more of in your life?

Plant a seedling together with your family. Each take turns to be responsible for looking after it, remembering to water and feed it as needed. Note its growth rate and appreciate the wonder of nature.

Spend some time today goal-setting as a family. What would you like to accomplish over the next week? Do you have any longer-term goals for the coming months? Write these down and remember to monitor your progress as you move towards your objectives.

Think of your fellow mom friends. Take a moment to appreciate their support and companionship. Write down five ways they nurture you as a mother, and five ways you could strengthen the bond even further.

Show your child how much you love them today in gestures rather than words. This could be setting aside time to hear about their day, reading together, or cooking their favorite meal. How did this make you feel?

_____

_____

_____

_____

_____

_____

_____

_____

_____

_____

_____

_____

_____

_____

_____

_____

_____

_____

If you could add a few hours to your day, how would you spend the extra time?

Take a few minutes to think about your relationship with your child. Are there any areas you'd like to improve? What steps can you take to bring you closer together?

What do you most dread?

Think back to the last week and list five things you are grateful for.

Which character from a children's story do you most relate to?

How confident are you?

Which character traits do you share with your child and how are you different?

Go screen-free for a day. Switch off the TV and place your cell phones and tablets out of reach. Read books, play games, get outside if you can. How was it for you? Could you commit to doing this once a week?

Play a game you enjoyed during your own childhood with your family today. How did it go? Did everyone enjoy it? Could this be a regular activity?

How good are you at making the best of a bad situation? Sometimes being a mom can mean turning lemons into lemonade. How easy do you find this?

Do something special for yourself today. This could be setting aside time to meditate, going for a run, or watching your favorite movie. Take pleasure in spending time with yourself and jot down ideas for future "me" activities.

Do you feel well supported? Are there any areas of your life where you'd like others to pick up the slack?

Who would play you in a movie about your family?

How resilient are you?

Finish the sentence: if I had one wish, it would be…

Are you like your own mother or other close female relations? Note down five similarities and five differences.

Share something about yourself with your child that they didn't already know. How did they react?

Today you're going to switch chores and responsibilities with your partner or another adult family member. If they usually do the laundry, this becomes your job. If you usually play taxi service for sports practice, your partner takes this on. How was it?

Head out to your garden or local park. Look around at the trees, flowers, and wildlife—all co-existing in this space. Write down five words connected to nature.

Together with your child, both draw a picture of the first thing you think of that is associated with the color green. Did you draw the same thing?

What are your talents?

Is the grass greener?

How would you like to grow as a person? Are there any areas of your life you'd like to develop over the next few months?

Do something as a family that benefits others. You could litter pick, donate unwanted items to charity, or volunteer at a local soup kitchen. Take time to think about this experience and each describe the day using just one word.

Write a letter to your child explaining how grateful you are that they came into your life. Describe your feelings the first time you laid eyes on them, and how much joy they give you. Take a few moments to appreciate your special bond.

Talk to your child about their hopes and dreams. What do they most desire? How will they reach their goals? Were your aims similar when you were their age?

List everything you're good at. Be bold and don't hold back—this is your time to celebrate yourself. Return to this list whenever you're in need of a confidence boost.

List the first five things that come to mind when you read the following words:

Fun

Chaos

Achievement

Morals

Think about a favorite teacher or mentor from your childhood, and the effect they had on you. Write them a letter of thanks.

What was your favorite pastime when you were a child? Can you incorporate some elements of this activity into your life today?

Do you feel content?

What is the most amusing thing your child has ever said?

Write a funny note to your child and hide it somewhere to be discovered.

How comfortable are you with your financial situation? Are there any steps you could take to improve your circumstances? Set yourself achievable goals and encourage your family members to do the same.

What causes the most disagreements in your family? Are there any changes you could make to help bring harmony to your home life?

How good are you at communicating your needs to others? Try to be upfront today and ask for help where you need it. Did you find it easy or was it a challenge?

_____

_____

_____

_____

_____

_____

_____

_____

_____

_____

_____

_____

_____

_____

_____

_____

_____

_____

What is the greatest piece of advice you were given as a child?

Is there anything you've been putting off? This could be getting a medical checkup, tackling a tricky work project, or having a difficult conversation with someone. Make today the day when you complete this task.

Who do you most admire, and has this changed over the course of your life?

Finish the sentence: If I could change one thing about my life…

What do you do to relax?

_____

_____

_____

_____

_____

_____

_____

What has surprised you most about motherhood?

_____

_____

_____

_____

_____

_____

_____

_____

Ask your child to describe you in no more than five words.

What makes you stressed?

Write a letter for your child to read ten years from now.

What's the story behind your child's name(s)? Do they have special meaning to you?

The next time your child is having a hard time, lie down on the ground with them. Take a few deep breaths and allow your bodies to become heavy. Encourage your child to feel supported by the ground beneath them, and by your presence.

List five things you've said to your child that you vowed to never say as a parent.

Has your view of your own mother changed since having your own child? Do you appreciate her more?

What is your favorite time of day with your child and why?

What are your highest priorities and how have they changed since becoming a mom?

How good are you at saying no?

Note the qualities you value in your child.

Think about how motherhood has changed you. Have you changed for the better? What do you miss about your life before becoming a mom?

Spend today being completely in the moment with your child, without distractions from work, chores, or electronic devices. Don't dwell on the past or worry about the future—your focus should be on the here and now. Was this a challenge?

List five things about yourself that would surprise your child if they knew.

Ask yourself how you can bring moments of joy to your day. This could be as simple as enjoying your morning coffee in peace, lighting a scented candle while you bathe, or phoning a friend you haven't spoken to for a while.

Who do you turn to for support? Having a network of trusted supporters around us can be reassuring in times of need.

Who are your parenting role models and how have they influenced you as a mother?

List the positives about reaching your current life stage.

List three things you wish you'd known as a new mom.

_____

_____

_____

_____

_____

_____

_____

What do you really love doing?

_____

_____

_____

_____

_____

_____

_____

_____

What's the biggest lie you've ever told your child?

Finish the sentence: I am happiest when…

Are you an introvert or an extrovert? Has your personality type shaped your parenting style?

_____

_____

_____

_____

_____

_____

_____

_____

_____

_____

_____

_____

_____

_____

_____

_____

_____

_____

_____

Consider how your day is governed by time and the need to "get things done." How would your day differ if you had no concept of time?

_____

_____

_____

_____

_____

_____

_____

_____

_____

_____

_____

_____

_____

_____

_____

_____

_____

_____

_____

List your most treasured memories. Close your eyes and allow yourself to relive these precious moments.

Look at a favorite family photograph. Spend a few moments examining it closely, taking in the scene. Allow your mind to wander back to the day it was taken and imagine yourself in that moment once again. How do you feel?

Take time to be calm in an otherwise busy day. Seek out a quiet spot and allow your mind to be quiet for a few minutes and note the effect on your mood.

What are your dreams for your child? Do they tally with their own aims and wishes?

What advice would you give your younger self?

Think back to your own childhood. What did you want to be when you grew up? Are there any similarities to your life now?

Channel your inner child today. Be playful, act on impulse, and be completely in the moment. Did this come naturally or feel a little strange?

_____

_____

_____

_____

_____

_____

_____

_____

_____

_____

_____

_____

_____

_____

_____

_____

_____

_____

_____

Think about something you rely on that you didn't have when you were a child—this could be your cell phone, your daily coffee fix, or your ability to drive—and go without it for a day. How did you cope?

Do you get enough sleep? Try a sleep detox tonight—remove all electronic devices from your bedroom, assign someone else to tend to your children if they wake, and take time to wind down before bed. Night night.

Did having a child affect your career? Has your work life moved in a different direction since becoming a mom? Is there anything you could do to achieve a better work-life balance?

Spend some time today thinking about your family traditions. Have these been passed down to you by your own parents? Could you create some new traditions?

Is there anyone in your life who drains you emotionally? How can you disengage from them to allow you time to focus on those who enrich you?

Reflect on your journey to motherhood. Perhaps it was an easy ride or there may have been bumps and unexpected turns in the road. Write down three words that best describe that time in your life.

Would you want to swap places with your child and grow up in today's world? Think about what it must be like to belong to the younger generation.

Spend time thinking about your mother's mother or an older female family member. Are you alike? Did she have more or fewer children? How were her experiences of motherhood different to yours?

Are you guilty of overplanning? Try spending today going with the flow, with no agenda or purpose. How did the day work out?

To what extent does your own child have more or fewer opportunities than you did at their age?

Think back to when your child was very small and you'd be awake during the night to feed and tend to them. What would you tell that tired new mom now if you could go back in time?

What mantra do you live by?

_____

_____

_____

_____

_____

_____

_____

_____

Do children have an easy ride today compared to previous
generations?

_____

_____

_____

_____

_____

_____

_____

_____

Write down your first thought on finding out you were going to be a mother.

Make a note of roughly how many hours per week you spend on various tasks—e.g. work, chores, exercise, hobbies, pastimes, watching TV. Are you happy with the balance? Would you like to devote more time to other activities?

How honest are you with your child? Do you sometimes hide the truth to spare their feelings?

Try to eliminate mental clutter today. Avoid reading, watching, or listening to anything that makes you feel stressed or anxious. If possible, steer clear of people who drain your energy, and instead engage in activities that enliven you. How was it?

Is there a hobby or pastime that you haven't devoted much time to since becoming a mom? Make a plan for how you can find the time to reignite this passion.

_____

_____

_____

_____

_____

_____

_____

_____

_____

_____

_____

_____

_____

_____

_____

_____

_____

How would you like to be remembered?

What has your child taught you?

Be a wellbeing warrior today. Teach your child the importance of self-care and model acts of personal kindness.

Describe your relationship with your own mother or a close female relative in no more than ten words.

Spend time today with someone who makes you laugh. Allow yourself to laugh freely without inhibition and note the effects on your body and mind.

How materialistic are you? Honestly appraise how important material possessions are to your sense of happiness and fulfilment. Does your child share your view?

Think of a time in your life when you have made a mistake or taken the wrong path. Forgive yourself and focus on how this experience has shaped you as a mother.

Imagine a time when your child is grown and has a family of their own. What sort of grandmother would you like to be? Note input you have found helpful from your own mother, mother-in-law, or close female friend.

Do you want your child to follow in your footsteps?

What does "home" mean to you?

List the greatest lessons you have learnt during your lifetime and reflect on their impact on you as a mother.

To what extent do you like to be in control? Are you typically the decision-maker in your family, or do you leave this to someone else? Would you like to have more or less responsibility for this going forward?

_____

_____

_____

_____

_____

_____

_____

_____

_____

_____

_____

_____

_____

_____

_____

_____

_____

Sit quietly with your child and encourage them to focus on their breathing. Can they notice the air entering their nose and lungs? Are there any changes in their body as they exhale? Continue mindfully breathing with them for a few minutes.

Do you find it easy to express your emotions or are you someone who holds your feelings in? Think of very young children who typically express themselves freely. What lessons can you learn from their behavior?

Today is all about celebrating achievements. Ask each family member to choose a recent accomplishment they are proud of, then spend today honoring these milestones.

Have a decluttering day! Encourage the whole family to join you in clearing out any items that are no longer useful or necessary and recycle them or donate them to charity. Congratulate yourself on making space, both literally and mentally.

Think of those who have guided you since becoming a mother. List the ways they have helped you on your parenting journey and take a moment to be thankful for their presence in your life.

Is it possible to balance achievement with kindness?

Who or what is your greatest inspiration?

Today try to concentrate on one task or activity at a time. Avoid multitasking, limit distractions, and allow yourself to focus. Did this come naturally to you?

Try taking a child's approach to a grown-up problem. Think of a recent difficulty or setback in your life and consider what a child might do in this situation. Did it throw new light on the issue?

Take a moment to consider your own happiness. Ask yourself, on a scale of one to ten, how happy you are in your life right now. If your score is lower than you'd like, consider how you can bring more enjoyment into your life.

What do you do to relax? Spend today making every task and activity as relaxing as possible—this could mean listening to soothing music while you work, spending some time on mindfulness exercises in between chores, and stretching before bed.

Are you holding on to emotional baggage? Close your eyes and let your mind settle on the event or experience. Allow yourself to feel the emotion for a few minutes, then gently let go of the emotion and come back to the present. Do you feel lighter?

What energizes you? Spend today on activities that invigorate your body and soul then write an account of your day.

Make a list of changes you'd like to make, regardless of whether it's within your power to do so. Now think about small steps you can take towards the bigger goals and make these small steps a reality.

What is the best gift you've ever received?

What are you preoccupied by?

What can you do today to nurture yourself? List some ideas to focus on your physical and mental wellbeing and try to incorporate as many as possible into your day.

Describe your perfect family day. Where would you go? Who would be present? Could you make this a reality?

Take some time today to connect with your spiritual self. Are there any spiritual practices you would like to begin or dedicate more time to? Is this something you could share with your child?

Write a few lines about a time in your life when you have felt strong. Bring those feelings of strength to the front of your mind and allow yourself to re-experience them in this moment.

List your magical moments from the last year. How do you feel looking back at these snapshots in time? Share your list with your child and relive these special times.

_____

_____

_____

_____

_____

_____

_____

_____

_____

_____

_____

_____

_____

_____

_____

_____

_____

_____

_____

What makes a house a home?

_____

_____

_____

_____

_____

_____

_____

What is your proudest moment since becoming a mother?

_____

_____

_____

_____

_____

_____

_____

_____

Think of a time in your life when you have overcome adversity and imagine your child in the same situation. Write them a note of encouragement to help them navigate the path ahead.

What needs to happen for you to experience a "good day"? For many of us, a good day will be when we've got lots done. But what if a "good day" could be experienced by resting and restoring instead of doing?

Think of a time in your life when you have felt disappointed or let down, then write about the experience using only positive words. Read this back to yourself and consider if that has made you view the experience differently.

If you could go anywhere and experience anything with your child, what would you do? Let your imagination run wild!

Do you sometimes find it difficult to pay attention? Spend today listening more than talking. Was this easy for you or did it feel strained?

Take your child for a walk in the rain. Feel the rain droplets on your skin, splash in puddles, and enjoy feeling free. Each think of three words to describe the experience.

Are you a patient person?

Is there a time in your life when dishonesty has caused conflict?

List your top five career challenges. What have these professional hitches taught you? What would you do differently? What advice would you give your child in the same situation?

List the first five things that come to mind when you read the following words:

Nature	Nurture

Freedom	Restraint

Rank the following in order of importance: money, career, family, love, fulfilment, stability, knowledge.

Describe your favorite place without naming it. Read the description to your family and see if they can guess the location. Ask them to do the same.

Think about your daily routines. Do you use your time efficiently?
Would you like to make any changes?

Are you curious? We tend to lose our natural sense of curiosity as we enter adulthood. Try spending today really exploring everything around you and see the world through your child's eyes. How was it?

Think back to your life before you had a child. Is there anything you wish you'd done more of, or anything you feel you spent too much time on?

Are you a strict parent?

What makes you happy?

What's the biggest secret you've ever been asked to keep? Did you manage to keep it to yourself or did you tell?

What qualities do you most admire in other mothers?

Do you sometimes agree to take on tasks or projects you really don't have the capacity for? Write a scenario where you politely decline. How does it make you feel?

Are you a good friend? Reflect on a time when you've helped someone through a difficult time, and also when you could perhaps have been more present.

Give some thought to your relationship with your body. Is it a positive one? Are you happy with the way you look? Write down five things you like about your body.

Stop what you are doing and take a moment to write a note to your child telling them how much they are loved.

_____

_____

_____

_____

_____

_____

_____

_____

_____

_____

_____

_____

_____

_____

_____

_____

_____

_____

_____

What's the bravest thing you've ever done?

Choose three words that best describe your personality.

Finish the sentence: The person I respect the most is...

Look at your face in a mirror. Study your skin, eyes, mouth, and nose closely. Notice how your face comes alive when you smile. Spend the rest of the day smiling whenever possible and note the effect this has on your mood.

Sit with your child and think about someone they would like to thank. Together write a letter or draw a picture expressing their gratitude. Send the letter or picture in the post.

Do you have a tendency to remove barriers for your child? Do you swoop to the rescue or prefer to let them figure things out for themselves? What would happen if you took the opposite approach?

Do you have a family pet? If so, write a story where your pet can talk and share it with your children.

Do you consider your life to be predictable? Shake things up by breaking away from the norm—do something completely out of character, wear clothes you'd never usually consider, take the opposite approach to a familiar situation. What did you learn?

Tell your mother or close female relation something you've always wanted to share with her but haven't found the words. If she's no longer with you, write her a letter and imagine her reading it.

What nicknames or terms of endearment have you used for your child over the years? Can you remember any of your own from your childhood?

Which quote from a book or movie most resonates with you?

What do you need to hear right now?

When was the last time you were amazed?

What is your earliest memory? Write it down and ask your child to share theirs.

What is your catchphrase? Ask your child and see if they agree.

How does your family celebrate Mother's Day? Would you like to do things differently?

When was the last time you cried? How comfortable are you with showing emotion in front of your children?

What annoys you most about your partner or closest friend? Do you feel comfortable asking them what annoys them most about you?

Think of a time when you've been frivolous. Was this a one-off or a regular occurrence?

Who do you adore?

How do you find peace?

What are your favorite smells? Do they evoke special memories?
How do they make you feel?

Write a nursery rhyme about a favorite trip or holiday with your family.

Play your child a favorite piece of music, then listen to theirs. Are they from similar genres or completely different?

Do you ever feel overwhelmed by the mental load of motherhood? Could you delegate tasks to lighten the load?

How do you start your day? Do you follow the same routine every morning? Could you try doing things differently?

What's your superpower?

What can you not get through the day without?

What has been your most useful purchase since becoming a mom?

To what extent are you a perfectionist? Could you take an "it'll do" approach once in a while or does this fill you with dread?

What does freedom mean to you? How comfortable are you with giving your child freedom (appropriate to their age)? Do they have more or less freedom than you did at their age?

Think back to your childhood friends. Are you still in touch with any of them? If not, would you like to be?

What has been the greatest challenge of your life? Is your child likely to face similar challenges? What advice would you give them?

What do you never want to forget?

What is the most beautiful thing you've ever seen?

Gather your family and each write down the name of your street or apartment block. Can you rearrange the letters to spell other words? Does the word have a certain meaning to you? Can you each pick a letter and think of a silly sentence beginning with that letter?

Write about an event or experience in your life that went unexpectedly well. Share this with your children and ask them to do the same. What did you learn from this?

_____

_____

_____

_____

_____

_____

_____

_____

_____

_____

_____

_____

_____

_____

_____

_____

_____

_____

Ask your child what they want to be when they grow up. Are there any similarities with your own childhood dreams?

Make a playlist for your child. You could include songs they like, tracks that remind you of them, or tunes that are important to your family. How did they react?

Create a family mood board. Every day for a week add images, drawings, or cuttings that represent milestones, events, and emotions. At the end of the week look at your mood board. How was the week for you? Is there anything you'd like more or less of?

Do you enjoy your own company?

_____

_____

_____

_____

_____

_____

_____

Are you and your partner on the same page?

_____

_____

_____

_____

_____

_____

_____

_____

Ask your child to appraise your performance. Get them to role play being your line manager and take you through a review meeting. What targets will they set you for the coming quarter?

List all of the places you've lived during your lifetime. Perhaps you've moved every few years or have always lived in the same town. Think about how well rooted you feel in your current home.

Write about a grudge you're holding on to. Think about how it's affected you, and why you can't let it go. Would your load be lighter if you could make amends and move on?

Finish the sentence: The person in my life who knows me best is…

What are your guilty pleasures?

Do you procrastinate?

What is your favorite memory of your school days?

Have you fulfilled your potential?

What five things would you save if your house was on fire?

Ask your child what they would do if they were president for a day.
What would you do?

Do you wake at night with your mind racing? Try keeping this journal next to your bed and note down anything that's troubling you.

What was your most embarrassing moment?

Do you act on impulse or are your actions careful and considered? Does this differ from your partner and/or child?

What three things would you do if you absolutely couldn't fail?

What one thing would make your life better?

How do you want to be remembered?

What has been your greatest adventure so far? How do you encourage your child to be adventurous?

Today is random acts of kindness day! Together with your family, spend the day making things a little bit better for others and the world around you.

Think of a time in your life when events have taken an unexpected turn. How easily did you adapt to the changing circumstances?

Write a letter to your ten-year-old self. What would you tell yourself if you could go back in time?

What are you avoiding?

What does being humble mean to you?

Is there someone you didn't get to say goodbye to? Say goodbye now, even if they can't hear you. Tell them how they impacted your life, and why you miss them. How did this feel?

Is there anything you learnt from your own mother or a close family member that didn't seem significant at the time, but ended up being valuable later on? Could you pass this on to your own child?

What values do you live by, and to what extent were these passed down by your parents? Is it important that your child shares the same values?

What is your favorite family rainy day activity? Can you think of other pastimes for the next wet weekend?

_____

_____

_____

_____

_____

_____

_____

_____

_____

_____

_____

_____

_____

_____

_____

_____

_____

_____

_____

_____

Are you in charge of your own destiny?

What really riles you up?

Write the age of your child, then think back to when you were a similar age. What similarities are there between their day to day activities and yours at their age?

Do you believe in luck? Think about times in your life when you have felt lucky, and times when luck wasn't on your side.

Finish the following sentences for your child:

You are as funny as …

You are as kind as …

You are as unique as …

You are as beautiful as …

Imagine you have been asked to give a talk to a group of expectant parents. List the top three things you wish someone had told you when you were in their shoes.

Do you or your child regularly experience feelings of anxiety or low mood? Try tracking your or their feelings hourly for a few days to see what might trigger these feelings.

What were the best and worst new baby gifts you received?

Are you pro-active or reactive?

What are your ambitions?

Write the word MOTHER vertically with each letter on a separate line. Think of a word beginning with each letter to describe your parenting journey so far.

What does your child call you? Are you always "mom" or has your child found their own name for you? Did they call you something different when they were small?

_____

_____

_____

_____

_____

_____

_____

_____

_____

_____

_____

_____

_____

_____

_____

_____

_____

_____

Do you believe in tough love? Is this something you practice with your own child?

Write a poem on the theme of Mother's Day.

Ask yourself how realistic your expectations are. Do you sometimes aim too high and feel disappointed when things don't work out as you'd hoped?

Spend a few minutes thinking about what it means to be a mother.
Write down every word or phrase that comes to you, then highlight
those that most relate to you in this moment.

Which has the most influence on your child: nature or nurture?

What are your victories?

What's on your bucket list?

Do you feel mothers sometimes get a raw deal? This could be professionally, politically, or socially. Are there any ways, no matter how small, that you could be a force for change?

What three things would you miss the most if you were stranded on a desert island?

Share a favorite book, story, or poem from your own childhood with your child. What did they think of it?

Note down the first thought that enters your head on waking every day for a week. At the end of the week read back over your thoughts. Are there any patterns? What do your thoughts say about you?

When did you know that you wanted to be a mom? Have you always wanted children or was becoming a mother a happy surprise? Did you plan to have more or less children than you have now?

If you could wake up tomorrow morning to find something major has changed in the world, what would you wish that change to be and how would it affect you?

Did you have an imaginary friend when you were young? Does your child have make-believe buddies? Imagine your mythical friends are real for the day. Where will you take them?

If you could be a parent in any decade, which would you choose and why?

Have fun with your child today by asking them silly questions in the style of a serious job interview. What would make a better pet, a robot or a dinosaur? Would they rather be as tall as a giraffe or as small as an ant? Is invisibility more useful than mind reading?

Imagine yourself 20 years from now. Write down everything you hope to have achieved, where you want to be living, and what your life will look like. How will you make this a reality?

Do you prefer being the parent or being the child?

What is your favorite season and why?

What would be in your ideas care package? Could you put this together for yourself to be used in times of need?

Dance with your child today. Put on some music you all enjoy and really let go. How did it feel?

Imagine you've been handed $50 to spend on anything you like. What would you buy?

Spend time alone with your child this week, without any siblings or other adults around. Choose a time when you can focus on them completely, without being distracted by your cell phone or other commitments. How was it?

What makes your child unique?

Teach your child one important life skill today. This could be how to do the laundry, prepare a meal, or write a letter. Could you make this a regular weekly activity?

Imagine you are going on a trip without your family. What key things would those covering for you at home need to know?

_____

_____

_____

_____

_____

_____

_____

_____

_____

_____

_____

_____

_____

_____

_____

_____

_____

_____

_____

Do you have any questions that need answering?

What have you bought that turned out to be completely useless?

Are there any affirmations that have special meaning to you? Could you share these with your child?

Make a list of fun, no-spend family activities. Could you fly a kite, bake cookies, make a collage? See how many you can come up with.

Imagine your family swapped places with a family living on the other side of the world. How well would you adapt? What new skills would you need to learn? Which routines would change and which would stay the same?

How were you disciplined as a child? Were these methods effective? Do you use the same strategies with your own child or have you developed your own techniques?

How compliant are you?

_____

_____

_____

_____

_____

_____

_____

What makes you, you?

_____

_____

_____

_____

_____

_____

_____

_____

To what extent do you stand up for your beliefs, even if others around you disagree? Would you want your child to do the same?

Take your child outside after dark on a clear night and look up at the sky. Which constellations and planets can you see? Can you see any pictures or patterns? Imagine how it must feel to be an astronaut.

Where do you fall in hierarchy with your siblings, if you have any?
Are you the oldest, middle, youngest, or only child? How do you
think this has shaped your personality?

_____

_____

_____

_____

_____

_____

_____

_____

_____

_____

_____

_____

_____

_____

_____

_____

_____

_____

_____

Imagine you could be anyone or anything you wanted for one day only. Who or what would you choose?

Are you a perfectionist?

If rebellion is the answer, what is the question?

Tell your partner or closest friend something you've never told anyone before. Were they surprised? Was it good to share this information or experience?

Think back to your teenage years. Were you happy? Did you have any worries or anxieties? What advice would you give to a teenager today?

Gather your family together and each take it in turns to write a line of a story that begins, "One day our family went on an adventure." Where will your imaginations take you?

Write a letter to someone you've encountered in your life who doubted your abilities. What do you want them to know about your accomplishments and achievements? What effect did their doubt have on you?

Does magic exist?

How important is conformity?

What app do you use the most and what does this say about you?

Ask yourself honestly how happy you are with your current relationship status. If you're single, does this suit you or would you like to be in a partnership? If you're in a long-term relationship, is this strong or are there cracks beneath the surface?

Were you a good student? Did you achieve everything you wanted academically? How important is it that your own child get good grades?

Look up today's horoscopes for each member of your family. Are there any accuracies?

What makes you attractive?

Who are you jealous of and why?

What worries you the most?

_____

_____

_____

_____

_____

_____

_____

What makes you feel empowered?

_____

_____

_____

_____

_____

_____

_____

Today you're going to play the lyric game! Ask each member of your family to think of a line from a song, then at some point today they have to say this line in a sentence and see if anyone notices.

Have you learnt to accept your flaws or are you preoccupied with trying to hide them? Do you find it easy to encourage your child to love their flaws instead of striving for perfection?

Set up a good deeds jar in your home. Every time someone in your family does a good deed place a marble or counter into the jar. When the jar is full, reward yourselves with a special family meal or day out.

What are your top parenting hacks?

Do you care what other people think?

How strong are you?

Is there a time in your life when you've been unkind to someone and regretted it? Did you find it easy to apologize? Share this experience with your child.

Spend today imagining you are a small child experiencing the world for the very first time. Did this change your enjoyment of your every-day activities?

Set your alarm for before dawn and take your family outside to watch the sunrise. Despite happening every day, sunrises are full of wonder. Ask each family member to describe the experience in no more than five words.

What would you call a reality TV show about your family?

What was the last compliment you received?

What are you really good at?

Write down your child's greatest talents. How can you nurture their creativity?

Think about your child's most used words and phrases. Are there any words that didn't exist when you were a child? Have fun writing dictionary entries for their expressions.

Ask your child to imagine an alien has landed in your yard and you need to explain how to live on earth. What's the first thing they'd teach it?

What hashtag would you give to today and why?

Do you find it easy to stay calm?

What would you choose: time or possessions?

Are there any personal habits you'd like to change? How can you hit the reset button?

How are you today? Are you feeling well and energized, or sluggish and downbeat? Is there a particular reason for these feelings? Do you need to redress the balance?